THE BEAST OF TIMES

THE BEAST OF TIMES

Adelina Anthony
with a contributing monologue by D'Lo

Foreword by Stacy I. Macías, Ph.D.

Kórima Press

Copyright © 2014 Adelina Anthony

All rights reserved. No portion of this work may be reproduced, performed, recorded, copied or otherwise transmitted in any form or by any means without written permission from the author or publisher except for small excerpts for educational or journalistic purposes.

Cover Photographer of Adelina Anthony and D'Lo: Marisa Becerra
Cover Design: Katie Poltz
Cover Background Photograph: "Mist in Kinabalu Jungle," by Antoine Hubert. Common license via Fotopedia
Book Design: Lorenzo Herrera y Lozano

Photo Credits:
Catalina and Lady Frijol (Scene 1) - *Marisa Becerra*
Bull (Scene 2) - *Marisa Becerra*
Catalina and Elk (Scene 3) - *Adam Earle*
Chicken (Scene 4) - *Adam Earle*
Bird and Fish (Scene 5) - *Adam Earle*
Cockroach and Lady Frijol (Scene 6) - *Marisa Becerra*
Cockroach (Scene 7) - *Adam Earle*
Catalina and Turtle (Scene 8) - *Marisa Becerra*
Rat (Scene 9) - *Adam Earle*
Lady Frijol and Bunny (Scene 10) - *Adam Earle*
Catalina (Scene 11) - *Marisa Becerra*
Coyote and Lady Frijol (Scene 12) - *Marisa Becerra*
Catalina and Lady Frijol (Scene 13) - *Marisa Becerra*
Catalina's stuffed dog - *Adam Earle*

Published by Kórima Press
San Francisco, CA
www.korimapress.com

ISBN: 978-0-9889673-6-6

*For the future generations who will build on our mistakes
and triumphs; may you keep the lucha going,
but never at the expense of your spirits or
compassion toward each other*

CONTENTS

Foreword by Stacy I. Macías, Ph.D. ix

Acknowledgements xv

Production History xxi

Scene One:	"Fighting like Colonized Cats & Dogs"	5
Scene Two:	"I Am Holy, Idiots" *	13
Scene Three:	"Pet Therapy"	19
Scene Four:	"Southern Fried Chicken"	27
Scene Five:	"Slickster"	33
Scene Six:	"Dog in Movement"	41
Scene Seven:	"What! What!"	49
Scene Eight:	"Soul Memory"	55
Scene Nine:	"Rat Race"	63
Scene Ten:	"Raising the Queer Bar"	69
Scene Eleven:	"Homegrown Resistance"	75
Scene Twelve:	"Distant Relations"	79
Scene Thirteen:	"This Bridge Called Home"	85

Bio: Adelina Anthony cxiv

Bio: D'Lo cxvi

FOREWORD

Humanity is for the Dogs: Pussies, Bitches, & a Queer Chicana Cultural Politics of Eco-Interdependence

Stacy I. Macías

In June 2013, I was lucky and wise enough to be an attendee at the first full-fledged production of Adelina Anthony's play, *The Beast of Times*. Since a 2001 UCLA queer Chicana/o arts symposium, I have enthusiastically seen just about every Anthony performance ranging in locations from Los Angeles to San Francisco to Austin. Given that Anthony's performance art oeuvre has been tuned to the politically, socially, and culturally conscious-minded, the title of her latest incarnation bewildered me; there was no particularly telling racial or sexual signifiers to ground my expectations or bespeak of my desire to see queer Chicana discourse unabashedly flung at an audience ready for the taking. In fact, I was puzzled. How would "beasts" be brought to life and deployed to comment upon our neoliberal-privatizing-education-times, our post-Obama/post-racial order politics, or our homo-nationalist-gay-marriage campaigning-hegemony—all themes and topics that Anthony illuminates in her work with astute thought and sharp humor.

To be clear, I have never identified as an animal lover or an environmental rights activist and have often prided myself on being one of those rare dykes to not own or even like cats. In short, I was not titillated at the thought of seeing a performance titled *The Beast of Times*, even with Adelina Anthony's name attached. When Anthony and D'Lo appeared on stage costumed as animals, I wondered: Has this Jota finally gone loca off the deep end??! Why turn to animal personifications to say something savvy and sublime about our current critical state? Was there no longer on-stage space for queer Chicanas to occupy? How ever could beastly themes or anthropomorphizing the animal kingdom breathe new life into queer Chicana politics, interlocking modes of oppression, and our demoralizing social order???

Upon *viewing* the play, the answer became clear.

By embodying animal subjectivities, Anthony adjusts our frames of reference and lovingly forces us to ditch our learned species hierarchy and engage in a kind of anthropological practice by looking at our humanity through the eyes of wounded, resilient animal others. The play is premised upon a smart analogy between the human world and the animal kingdom in which subjectivized animals encounter their reality with consciousness, acuity, and compassion through fully realized sexual, gender, racial, and class-based identities, all of which form an amalgamation that historically and scientifically speaking has only been reserved for the human species to inhabit. Caught up in the sheer humor of imbibing two respected performance artists, Adelina and D'Lo, embody the behaviors and simulate the sounds of a cat and a dog engaged in witty repartee, I was not ready for the fuller range of responses that the play would additionally elicit from me including outrage, heartbreak, pleasure, and conviction. Watching animal others quip, testify, and hold each other accountable on stage was as much a self-reflexive, heady, and ruminating exercise as it was a delightful escape into a raunchy yet all-ages friendly production.

Upon *reading* the play, the answer also became complicated.

Structurally, the play consists of a series of vignettes narrated by domesticated pets, farm animals, and an insect, all of whom collectively comprise the otherworldly place subtending human-centered society and embody what I would call "animality"— an equivalent of humanity designed and inhabitable for all animal species. In this parallel universe, we first meet Miss Lady Frijol, as Dog, and Catalina, the Spanish-identifying, colonized Gatita whose budding politics will arrive through the act of remembering—a process that happens on and through the body to remind us of that powerful pre-modern mode of knowledge making and sharing that takes hold of us emotively and to our collective benefit. And as Gloria E. Anzaldúa reminds us, once we know, we can never go back to not knowing.

Through the creation of a bona fide society replete with animal subjects (rather than objects) who think, speak, and feel, Anthony brilliantly exposes the utility and transferability of Queer Chicana politics, theories, and productions to additional worlds and beings. Over the last few years, new trends in interdisciplinary scholarly thought, including critical animal studies, food studies knowledge, and eco-feminism, have emerged. Concurrent with these emergences in institutions of learning have been the elision of Chicana feminist thought, the characterizations of women of color feminism as antiquated—aptly described by gatita Catalina as "some last-century eighties notions of queer womyn of color feminisms"—and the steady de-funding and thus elimination of programs and departments, which were specifically formed to counter the erasure of people of color histories and non-dominant modes of inquiry. I read Anthony's queerly racialized animal world as one making new sense and use of Chicana feminist discourse for an audience seduced by the never-ending ascendance of "the new" while also reprising the "good ole" use of intersectionality to understand the interdependency of all sentient creatures.

In this way, ethical debates about non-human species, critical animal and food studies approaches, ecofeminism, environmental justice, and any other non-hierarchically invested frameworks of thought and being have much to lift and learn from Anthony's queer of color feminist pedagogy in *The Beast of Times*. In the least, sexy new scholarly formations can benefit from understanding that to speak about speciesism, agribusiness and foodways, ecologically sound conservation systems, and the global threat to our natural environment requires a fundamental understanding of interlocking structures of oppression, which queer women of color feminisms have long theorized and of which Anthony, through comical means, reminds us.

While the heart of the play beats to the rhythm of animal life—assuredly serving to interrogate the natural order of things like heteronormative human time and space—*The Beast of Times* also provides explicit and effective critiques of humanity and animality, and thus the aspirations that can ravage all beings in their quests for love, justice, and the divine. Moreover, by implicitly critiquing that the US government has deemed corporations as beings with the same rights as humans, Anthony's queer cast of animals stage urgent interventions into the most harrowing issues of our contemporary political scenes. As the head lawyer roach for the Law of Mother Earth Trial, Ms. Cuca Racha proclaims, "...human institutions must be interrogated at all levels." In other scenes, we are reminded of histories disappeared at the hands of official narratives (Grandma Tanzanian Tortoise and elder Native American Coyote), present lives still hanging in the balance (working-poor Chicken of color and Trinidadian Rat), and futures neither extinguished or yet materialized (Catalina and Lady Frijol). Fittingly, the words of Charles Dickens's opening lines from his novel, *A Tale of Two Cities*, picked up in the title of Anthony's *The Beast of Times*, summons our current critical juncture: "It was the best of times, it was the worst of times…we were all going direct to Heaven, we were all going direct the other way." So if all dogs [read: Dog, or Miss Lady Frijol] go to heaven, where may that leave the rest of us?

I'd like to image that as the conscience of the play, Miss Lady Frijol represents our better selves' utmost desires to abandon our cozy homes of comfort, our security blankets and bones, and the plans to which we have become loyal in favor of boldly stepping out and taking a stance against the quotidian violences we witness and are implicated in daily. Ultimately, *The Beast of Times* captures a society of humans and animals much more like each other than not in order to advocate for eco-worlds that are centered on building horizontal relationships of respect and interdependence. New earths informed by queer Chicana feminist imaginings. And leave it to Anthony to lead the gloriously untamed way there.

Stacy I. Macías
January 16, 2014
Las Vegas, NV

ACKNOWLEDGMENTS

This artistic endeavor has been greatly supported once more by beautiful friends, audiences, and organizations. *The Beast of Times* may never have come about were it not for the encouragement of Sarah Guerra, the former Program Coordinator at La Peña Cultural Center in Berkeley, CA. Through her invitation on behalf of La Peña, I applied for a National Performance Network (NPN) Creation Fund. I applied in 2009 and when I was not awarded the grant, it was through her insistence I re-applied the following year for my solo project. But by the end of 2010, I had exhausted the solo form for myself. Thankfully, the Creation Fund allowed me to re-imagine the work from a solo play to two-person play. I am grateful to NPN for administering an award that truly allows for artist process and understands the process may take us in new directions altogether.

Fortunately, one of my dearest amigos is the talented D'Lo. For those of you who know D'Lo as a performer you are already aware of his generosity of spirit and heart—these are the same qualities he brings into any creative environment. I could not imagine another queer/trans person of color to share the stage with in this play. The success of its development and premiere are highly indebted to him and our fruitful collaboration process.

The initial development of the play was also greatly informed by the intimate reading I conducted in my Oakland living room for Marisa Becerra and Cherríe Moraga. They had the grace and patience to sit through a sprawling, ambitious work. That evening of honest feedback from both of them gave me the clarity to move forward with the work as a writer. I thank them again for allowing me to read the work in its earliest of stages when we had so many animals in the script it felt like a zoo.

A couple of months later we were finally rehearsing the play on its feet at La Peña. La Peña staff went beyond my expectations as a commissioner, providing access to space and extra rehearsal hours. Gracias especially to Sarah, Paul Chin, Mariola Fernandez, Fernando "Feña" Torres, and other staff and volunteers always ready to lend a hand during our performances.

A week before our official residency at La Peña we cornered our friend Denise Contreras and forced her to sit through a reading of the play. She seemed to enjoy herself, smiling, laughing, and shaking her head every now and then at our antics. I am thankful for her years of friendship and how she proved herself a loyal friend more than once by turning down tempting bribes to "let the cat out of the bag."

During our NPN residency week we had the critical eye and directorial skills of Mark Valdez. His dramaturgical questions pushed the script forward and he added polish to our characterizations and performance. Moreover, his infectious energy and bubbly personality created a playful environment we enjoyed immensely as performers. Thank you, Mark, for having the faith to join us in this zany adventure and for always coming back to us during reprisals to improve our performances.

As an artist in conversation with my communities, I couldn't have been more grateful for the Berkeley audiences we encountered our first weekend, including our preview audience. The show grew every night because of their responses and feedback. Gracias to Anjali Alimchandani for helping with the specificity of dialect for the *Bunny* monologue. I also thank Masami Kawai for the help around the *Fish* monologue. Finally, special gratitude for Serian

Strauss who implored me to ensure her continent was represented, thus inspiring the creation of *Grandma Turtle*.

I also know those first audiences in the Bay Area were dazzled by the fabulous costumes designed by Marisa (Meowisa) Becerra. While I know my fiancé to be a woman of many talents, it was thrilling for me to have audiences discover her through her own inspired creations. Mil gracias, Marisa, for your "MexGyver" skills, and your quips like "agüantándome bay" and "*U-bunny-shads*." I am still amazed by what you can do with duct tape and a deadline. I remain enamored by your constant apoyo of my art and life. If I were a kitty, you'd be my catnip.

Four months later we were blessed to have another fantastic weekend of performances in Austin with our second co-commissioners, *allgo* (a Texas Statewide Organization for Queer People of Color). This second workshop was critical in allowing me to test out the new scenes I had written, especially the one with Catalina and the Grandma Turtle—which is the heart of the play. Our residency week with *allgo* was helmed by the phenomenal producer, Priscilla A. Hale. She also assembled a fantastic technical crew, which included Rose M. Pulliam who saved us by running the soundboard; gracias as well to the helpful staff at the Emma S. Barrientos Mexican American Cultural Center; and a huge thank you to Anjali for taking our photos and serving as an assistant stage manager that week; needless to say, D'Lo and I were both supported immensely by our respective partners during this week. Tlazocamtli to our audiences that weekend (even avowed non-animal lovers who went for the ride with us anyway). I want to give a special shoutout to Genevieve Rodríguez, mi amiga cubana, who gave feedback on the *Pig* monologue.

Six months later, we took the show to Los Angeles for a final workshop performance. This time I have to extend my gratitude to Kim Yutani, Kerri Stoughton-Jackson, and the rest of the Outfest Fusion Queer People of Color staff for coordinating this effort along with the L.A. Gay & Lesbian Center. Performing this final workshop production at the Renberg Theater allowed Jon Imparato to see our show, and we remain grateful he invited us that same evening to bring it back for a full production. True to his word, Jon assembled an incredible team to give us a dream world-premier production. We remain indebted to Matt Walker, Katie Poltz, Patricia Sutherland, Robert Selander, Shaunnessy Quinn, Bethany Tucker, Adam Earle, Sofia Barrett-Ibarra, Kathleen Jaffe, Karla Legaspy, Josh Allen Goldman, the box-office staff, the volunteers, and all of the Center Security Guards who were our best escorts ever. Special thanks to Karla and Lizzie Chaidez for coordinating to bring their high school students to a show and for additional outreach support.

During our run, several audience members touched our hearts by returning to see the show more than once, as did the audience members who traveled miles and from other parts of the country to see this play. This is why I/we do the work.

I am also indebted to the generous words provided by our "blurbistas." Thank you, Sheena Malhotra, José Manuel Aguilar-Hernández, and Kristina Wong. I am honored to know so many fierce queer/people of color academics and fellow ally artists. Gracias to all of my academic supporters and friends who encourage their students to see my/our works. Finally, I am beyond honored to have las palabras of Stacy Macías grace this published play with her thoughtful, forthright, beautiful, and astute foreword. Having presented my original works in L.A. for over thirteen years, she is one of those queer Xicana comadres who has been a faithful audience member and supporter

Finally, this published play you hold in your hands would not be possible without the vision, dedication, and commitment made by one of our own great literary talents, el Lorenzo Herrera y Lozano from Kórima Press. Hermano, knowing the time it takes to make these publications (future queer artifacts) possible makes your offering to our communities even more cherished. I remain utterly appreciative and only hope your own poetry finds its way into the hands and hearts of others. Thank you for everything you do to make this jota feel loved.

PRODUCTION HISTORY

This play was first conceived by Adelina Anthony as a solo work, "Jotalogues." Anthony was awarded a 2010 Creation Fund by the National Performance Network (NPN) and it was co- commissioned by La Peña Cultural Center and *allgo*, (a Texas Statewide Queer People of Color Organization. Later, as Anthony developed the concept of the "animal" world and saw the work's potential as a two-person play, she invited fellow performance artist D'Lo to collaborate. D'Lo contributes the monologue, "I Am Holy, Idiots," and was also key in the rehearsal process: contributing ideas, fine-tuning language and dialects, and creating characterizations.

This work was written for Adelina Anthony and D'Lo as the primary touring artists. However, for future independent productions this play may be cast with a larger ensemble to fit the needs of other directors and producers. (Music design may also be changed.)

This project was presented as a workshop production at La Peña Cultural Center in Berkeley, CA in May 2011, directed by Mark Valdez. Valdez was also a valuable collaborator during the NPN residency week at La Peña. Technical director and sound board operator was Sarah Guerra. Light board operator was Cris Ceballos. In September 2011, this project was presented with new scenes as another workshop production at The Mexican Cultural Center via *allgo* in Austin, TX; these performances were based largely on Valdez's direction with new scenes directed by Anthony. The lighting designer was Tomas Salas, light board operator was Richard Striebel, sound board operator was Rose Pulliam, assistant stage manager was Anjali Alimchandani, and the producer was Priscilla Hale. The final workshop production was presented in March 2012 in Los Angeles, CA, as part of the OUTFEST/FUSION 2012 Queer People of Color Film Festival at the Renberg Theater.

The play had its World Premiere on May 31, 2013, and closed on June 16, 2013, at the L.A. Gay and Lesbian Center's Renberg Theater.

Producer	Jon Imparato
Playwright	Adelina Anthony
	(w/contributing monologue by D'Lo)
Director	Mark Valdez
Performers	Adelina Anthony and D'Lo
Stage Manager	Kathleen Jaffe
Asst. Stage Manager	Sofia Barrett-Ibarra
Costume Design	Marisa Becerra
Light Design	Shaunessy Quinn
Stage Design	Robert Selander
Light Tech/Op	Adam Earle
Sound Tech/Op	Bethany Tucker

The musical selection was a collaborative effort between Adelina Anthony, Marisa Becerra, D'Lo, Anjali Alimchandani, Mark Valdez, and Bethany Tucker. Preshow music by Jon Imparato.

Current Running Time: 75 minutes (no intermission)

Setting/Set: Post-the latest world-crisis, today! This production has a minimalist approach and style. The set is comprised of an old trunk on stage with a giant stuffed dog on top of it. Different items are pre-set on stage: a huge dog bowl, a giant book (*This Bridge Called My Back*), and a guide cane with a bundle. The actors are dressed in black coveralls. Their animal characterizations come about through physical interpretation and small costume pieces (ears, tails, wings, etc.). The four testimonial monologues break the fourth wall.

CHARACTERS IN ORDER OF APPEARANCE
(A=Adelina/D=D'Lo):

CATALINA (A)	Female kitten, speaks with Spaniard accent
LADY FRIJOL (D)	Mature asexual canine with British accent
BULL (D)	Young South Asian bull trying to be a cow
ELK (D)	Conservative Lakota psychotherapist
CHICKEN (A)	Poor Southern middle-aged colored female
BIRD (D)	Chicano/Mexican "slickster"
FISH (A)	Gay Japanese elder on a mission
COCKROACH (A)	Jewish-Latina with a chip on her shoulder
PIG (A)	Playboy Cuban Miami cochino
TURTLE (D)	Ancient grandma from Tanzania
RAT (D)	Rat-ivist from Trinidad living in NYC
BUNNY (A)	Hyper-poly-pan-species-sexual Indian
COYOTE (A)	Homeless Native American coyote

SCENE ORDER

Scene One:	"Fighting like Colonized Cats & Dogs"
Scene Two:	"I Am Holy, Idiots" *
Scene Three:	"Pet Therapy"
Scene Four:	"Southern Fried Chicken"
Scene Five:	"Slickster"
Scene Six:	"Dog in Movement"
Scene Seven:	"What! What!"
Scene Eight:	"Soul Memory"
Scene Nine:	"Rat Race"
Scene Ten:	"Raising the Queer Bar"
Scene Eleven:	"Homegrown Resistance"
Scene Twelve:	"Distant Relations"
Scene Thirteen:	"This Bridge Called Home"

Monologue written by D'Lo

THE BEAST OF TIMES

SCENE ONE: FIGHTING LIKE COLONIZED CATS & DOGS

[*Classical music plays: "Movement 4: Tortoises" from Carnival of Animals by Camille Saint-Saens as the lights come up. We hear a woman call out, "Lady Frijol, Catalina... Treats!" LADY FRIJOL (DOG) and CATALINA (CAT) run across the stage, midway LADY FRIJOL stops. LADY FRIJOL starts packing. CATALINA returns with a treat.*]

CATALINA: ¿Qué va? You don't want your treat?

LADY FRIJOL: No, I'm not that kind of dog anymore.

CATALINA: (*Tempting him.*) Are you sure?

LADY FRIJOL: Quit fussing about. This is serious. Stop acting like a little pussy.

CATALINA: Naturaca de la vaca, it's my nature to be a pussy, not like you can just stop being a bitch.

LADY FRIJOL: Don't speak to me in that tone; I'm your elder.

(*CATALINA jumps on trunk and kneads her stuffed dog.*)

CATALINA: Elder? You're only older than me by seven dog years. You're not the boss of me.

LADY FRIJOL: C'mon, you scaredy-cat, come with me. I would've thought you'd be at least curious.

CATALINA: ¡Me cago en la leche! (*LADY FRIJOL responds with a sound.*) Have you seen the unnatural size of their ratones? I can't believe some felines actually eat those fast food supersized rodents. Meow, just the thought of it makes me... (*Starts hacking a hairball.*)

LADY FRIJOL: Rubbish. And who are you to judge body size? It's not natural for a cat to have bulimia.

CATALINA: I'm not bulimic! Hairballs.

LADY FRIJOL: Preserving some model figure, god only knows why. Look, pound kitty, you'll be spayed soon, so like me, you'll never get shagged.

CATALINA: I get laid plenty.

LADY FRIJOL: Your stuffed animals don't count. (*Begins to gather things.*)

CATALINA: Bitch, please. I mean, Miss Lady Frijol.

LADY FRIJOL: Fuck off, you're not allowed to call me that! (*Barks viciously. CATALINA swipes.*) You're such an asshole. (*Says the following line as the ultimate put down.*) You were probably a human in your previous lives! (*CATALINA meows painfully.*) I'm sorry. (*LADY FRIJOL tosses the ear-torn copy of* This Bridge Called My Back *onto the stuffed animal.*) Here you go. Read it, you lazy cat. You might learn something. I know I did. They don't teach us this in our dog schools.

CATALINA: Frijolito, I mean, Itzcui... Itzcui—

LADY FRIJOL: Say it! Say my original name from this continent.

CATALINA: Oh, god, you know Nahuatl doesn't flow naturally from my tongue.

LADY FRIJOL: Because it's colonized! It's pussy. Not puthy.

CATALINA: ¡Vale! Some of us call it progress. Look at your water bowl. Your cuppeth over floweth! (*She picks up the book and laughs.*) Meow! Lady Frijol, you're not seriously going to build a movement on some last century eighties notions of queer womyn of color feminisms?

LADY FRIJOL: Some of us animals believe in coalition building. Are you just going to idle about while the humans ruin our planet?!

CATALINA: This book is so old and water stained. What do people do with it? Masturbate?

LADY FRIJOL: Intellectually, yes, but... wait—have you even read it?

CATALINA: Hello, I'm just a kitten! Besides, I play plenty under the dinner table where I hear Judy and her university friends talk shop. Everybody knows we're living in a post-colonial, post-racial... post-mailman world.

LADY FRIJOL: Cor, I liked you better when they first brought you from Boyle Heights, just a defiant barrio gata with the potential for counter resistance chola-speak.

CATALINA: Don't go romanticizing poverty! You purebred liberal self-righteous Berkeley commie bitch! (*LADY FRIJOL attacks. CATALINA fights back.*) We're lucky to have lesbian owners like Sandra and Judy!

LADY FRIJOL: Exactly! We're just some privileged pets that got lucky. Do you even know how the economic recession has created a rise in animal kills at the local shelters?

CATALINA: Mala pata. Maybe they'll get lucky in their next life. Queers are adopting more these days. And being owned by a queer couple is heaven on earth.

LADY FRIJOL: No, Catalina! It's not! We're colonized, you daft uneducated cat! (*CATALINA swipes. They fight. LADY FRIJOL stops.*) Look at us. We don't even leave this huge carpeted and marbled home nestled in the Berkeley Hills. "I know why the caged bird sings."

CATALINA: Meow... (*rubbing her tummy*) me apetece.

LADY FRIJOL: (*Sighs like a wounded dog.*) Adiós, kitty. When they come looking for me, all I ask is that you don't sell me out... so quickly. I need at least a three hour lead so I can catch the BART to SFO to JFK with some PETA allies. I'm posing as a seeing eye dog.

CATALINA: But you're the blind one! No, perra, you can't go out there. You don't know your way around. Plus, I thought the DVD we watched with Judy and the kids was called *Lady and The Tramp*, not *Lady becomes The Tramp*. Meow. No, perra, please, don't leave me! It's a dog eat dog world.

LADY FRIJOL: Keep your internalized animalphobia to yourself. (*A dejected CATALINA meows. Beat.*) You take care of yourself, little one. And don't get too cozy with your creature comforts. Technically, you were adopted by Sandra, and we've both heard them going at it for months now.

CATALINA: Yeah, but, Sandra... Sandra can't leave Judy. How would she take care of me? She's... she's, you know—

LADY FRIJOL: A broke-ass lesbian. Precisely. (*About to exit. Says the following like a guerilla warrior in the making.*) In the spirit of animal solidarity, Catalina, I'm sorry I chewed up your favorite toy mouse when you first moved in and that I buried it somewhere in the back yard.

CATALINA: *You* did that to my mouse?

LADY FRIJOL: Yes, but I understand now that that's how this human establishment keeps us apart, and, furthermore, how they co-opt our social justice value systems. It's stupid to fight over territory we don't really own, and it's stupid to feel possessive and protective over a human *owner*. Adiós, kitty. I'm off to participate in the international court case of the century! I can't wait to see that celebrity attorney in action, Ms. Racha! (*Barks and then exits.*)

CATALINA: But... but you're a dog! What happened to your sense of loyalty? A man's best friend! (*Beat.*) Vale, there you have it, a *man's* best friend. Obviously, not a lesbian's!

(*CATALINA picks up the book, her stuffed toy dog, and exits. We hear a snippet of the song: "Who Let the Dogs Out" by Baha Men. Lights crossfade to a spotlight.*)

SCENE TWO: I AM HOLY, IDIOTS

[*BULL enters ringing his cowbell and dancing to the Baha Men song. He stands in the downstage spotlight.*]

BULL: (*With right hand raised.*) I won't swear cuz it's not nice, but, yes, I promise to tell the whole truth, so help me Ganesha. (*Lowers hand.*) So, ya, I'm gay. I'm so gay. You all can tell I'm gay, but for some it's not obvious. See over theya, in South Asia, ve can hold hands with other males and no vun thingk anything. Every bull does it, even the married ones. But it's true most married bulls want to partake in my brand of (*slaps his ass*)... holiness. But I got bored and had to leave all of that alone. So I came here... how do you ask? I am holy, idiots. I flew.

But here is so different. Such a different thing to be a "cow" here. At first, I didn't know what to do, the bulls were so big and muscular. I kind of likeded it. But it was strange. All over South Asia, you only find puny little bull-cows like me. Don't let my twinky self fool you, I am strong and I have a great capacity to hold a lot of weight. (*Winks and rings his bell.*)

So ya, the American bulls have good genes. Strong genes. Manifest Destiny genes. Ya, corn-fed genetic hybrid Wrangler genes. I remember my first American love. Stanley. It was the 2nd day I was here and I got bored with hanging with the cows all day, so I went over to the bull pen. That's where I saw him— what a stud. I went into the haystacks and hid and watched him for hours. I could see him flexing every white muscle and he must've felt my stare, because he turned around and then I got so scared because he could see that I wasn't a... cisgender cow. But thank Ganesha that instead of stampeding off or kicking my ass, he just smiled at me with his pretty blue eyes. And like the gay bull I discovered him to be... (*pulling out a red scarf*) it was as if I was covered in red silk, I could see the desire burning in his eyes and next thing you know, we were rolling around in the haystacks and I heard temple bells ring over and over and over. It was the first time I did pooja in public. He could go on forever, sometimes it was a real pain in my ass! All those drugs kept him feeling fabulous and craving me!

I did love all the attention I was getting. But what I didn't like was the fact that he kept trying to get *me* to shoot up. He said it made the sex better. Better than what we just did? I was so confused. And when I didn't agree to his druggie lifestyle, he apparently went around fucking other drugged up bulls. Eventually, I got sick of seeing him become more and more addicted to something that was supposed to make him feel good, even though it stripped him of who he really was... an organic Nebraskan cow. He said it wasn't his fault he was a druggie, that the humans from the meat packing industry had put the drugs in his body and it was the only way he could compete with the bigger and beefier bulls.

Ya, I realized gay American bulls, were no better than the ones in South Asia. Just using me for my… holiness. Why is it emotionally hard to connect with other gay bulls? Why do we have to party, party all the time? With Stanley, I wanted something more than just the roughness of sex. I almost left America, thinking I was just another young brown bull-cow for all the beefcakes. This is why I am here.

I wish I could say Stanley and I ended on good terms, but there was beef between us. I tried to warn him, "They're going to ask you to pay up for all those free drugs they're giving you." I didn't get to say goodbye. I heard his screams of terror and pain in the slaughterhouse. What could I do? I am just one puny little bull trying to be a cow. But this is why I am here. I will continue to share Stanley's story until justice is served. (*Beat.*) Thank you, your Honor.

(*We hear "Wind" by Native Flutescapes. Lights crossfade. The large stuffed toy dog is thrown on stage, CATALINA jumps on it as the other actor changes into the ELK behind the trunk.*)

SCENE THREE: PET THERAPY

[*CATALINA rambles and eventually ELK sits on the trunk smoking his Native pipe. He clears his throat when he hears profanity.*]

CATALINA: So if you ask me, doc, that's why *she* should be in here. Not me. I'm not the nutcase. I can't believe she just up and left us like that… for a movement. Who does that? She's always been an angry bitch.

ELK: Who is angry?

CATALINA: Lady Frijol—only the dog I've been complaining about the last ten minutes. Vale, for a therapist you don't have good listening skills. Can I be excused now?

ELK: (*Examining his watch.*) I'm afraid we have 35 minutes to go.

CATALINA: Is that in cat or elk time?

ELK: Human time.

CATALINA: Doc, you and I know human time is irrelevant. Tick-tock-tick-tock. Busy, busy, busy. Doing what? Posting cute pictures of kitties like me online? Did I tell you Judy made me a Facebook page the other day? Are you online, doc? Cause if you are I'll friend you. (*ELK yawns loudly.*) Why you got so many teeth missing?

ELK: Ah, the Lakota males are given elk tooth to promote long life.

CATALINA: Mala pata for you.

ELK: No, it is a great honor to be noticed for my virility. Males in all species, as you know, are the precious leaders, protectors of females, in a good way.

CATALINA: Not in my pussy world.

ELK: Now tell me more about Judy.

CATALINA: Judy is my sole owner now that Sandra's been kicked out.

ELK: And Sandra is…?

CATALINA: She's my *original* human owner, because before she moved here to the Bay Area to come to graduate school, she's the one who picked me out from Craigslist. But Judy's the one who's been paying for my medical expenses, boarding, grooming! Vale, I know who puts the catnip treats in my bed.

ELK: Hmmm.

CATALINA: Do you think that's materialistic of me, doc? (*ELK's "yes" is not even heard by CATALINA.*) No, it's not. Al pan pan y al vino vino, it's called loyalty. I didn't fuck up on Judy And I'm sure you've seen the flyers all over fucking Berkeley. Lost Dog. Big Reward.

	But if you ask me $1000 dollars is way too much to pay for that unfaithful bitch. (*He coughs again.*) Doc, you got a hairball?
ELK:	No, but I think you should stop—
CATALINA:	Good. So, listen, la pobre Judy, she's been so heartbroken over the loss of Lady Frijol. That's why I couldn't come out of hiding when Sandra was calling me to go with her and Mario.
ELK:	And who is Mario?
CATALINA:	Sandra's "friend" from her Berkeley school. The guy she cheated with. His name used to be Maria, but that was years before I was born.
ELK:	Oh. And how does this make you feel? (*CATALINA purrs and rubs herself against her stuffed dog. ELK clears his throat.*) Catalina. Catalina! How does it make you feel?
CATALINA:	Huh?
ELK:	That Sandra cheated on Judy… with a transman?
CATALINA:	Who's talking about cars?
ELK:	Nevermind.
CATALINA:	I mean, sure, Judy is a bit overbearing and mothering sometimes. She never lets her kids

THE BEAST OF TIMES

go outside by themselves. They were adopted like me. Come to think of it, Sandra couldn't go anywhere by herself either. (*Beat*.) Judy just cares a lot. Look at me. She's so worried I've been traumatized by the upheaval of the last week— I'm enrolled in six sessions of pet therapy. (*Starts to rub herself against ELK*.) But Judy's the one who's not been her organized self. I even heard her say she forgot to get me spayed. Whatever that means. (*Looks at ELK*.) Doc, did you know you kind of have that cute professor look going for you? But I'd bet you'd look a lot cuter if you didn't wear those owl ring glasses. They really only look good on owls. (*Purrs. As an aside*.) ¡Qué va! I'm falling in love with my therapist. (*CATALINA looks back at ELK*.) Being in heat really lowers the bar.

ELK: So, Catalina, why aren't you eating?

CATALINA: (*Licks herself*.) It's silly, doc. Bueno, do you really think it's possible the humans can destroy our world?

(*We hear "Wind" by Native Flutescapes*.)

ELK: Mmmm... as an elder elk, I remember the grandfathers told me the following story when I was just a young calf running wild and wrestling with other young males—

CATALINA: Meow!

ELK: (*Admonishing.*) No, Catalina! Because I had not found my harem of females yet! (*CATALINA decides to leave. He is unaware of her departure.*) When females want more than males and forget their place in the cosmos it is always dangerous. The same goes for males. I knew that sweating with two-spirited elk was only temporary. I knew I had a future duty to fulfill. I never questioned it... until I came across a Black Mamba snake. From Africa. (*ELK smiles slightly.*) Yes, a leather daddy... in a good way. (*ELK catches himself lost in his "illicit" memory. He clears his throat. *The following text is loosely based on a Lakota creation story.*) As I was saying, Catalina, there was a time when human females became so crazed that they neglected all things for the sacred dance. They even forgot their babies. Wives became mixed with wives, so that poor husbands did not know their own from others... (*Turns toward her.*) Another wasted session. (*Exits. Lights crossfade to spotlight.*)

SCENE FOUR: SOUTHERN FRIED CHICKEN

[*A CHICKEN enters squawking and talking as she walks into the downstage spotlight. She raises her hand.*]

CHICKEN: Lawd Jesus, don't get your feathers ruffled. I didn't come this far not to tell the truth. Cause lawd knows they don't give a damn about us colored chickens. Fuck the lack of no space and ventilation in the prison coop. Never mind the Southern heat is hot enough to melt your beak. And if you're not careful, you're bound to step on some chicken shit, or some chicken who done lost her head from heat exhaustion and done got deaded and died.

So, when you ask me, Ms. Racha, ma'am, if human technology has made it easier for animal life, I'm like, come spend a day in my drug infested projects and you'll get your answer first hand. (*Clucks*.) Ooh, lawd, from the projects to the prisons, all I ever seen is colored chickens. And this prison life is something altogether diabolical for colored females. Lawd, I can't tell you how many eggs I've laid in my lifetime. And do I get to see any of those chicks grow up? Hell nah. And you all think I'm getting knocked up in natural ways. (*Clucks*.) Day in, day out, we're surrounded by human guards and surveillance cameras. What kind of chance does a chicken have for a normal life? Whatever normal is. And, lookie here, we Houston poultry were having it rough enough, but after that damn Katrina, any lost or unclaimed chickens just got crammed up in there with us. (*She pushes away imaginary chickens and pecks hard.*)

Way I see it, times ain't really changed, especially when the Colonel can still make his profit off us colored chickens selling his cheap KFC buckets of cholesterol. And why would they care to improve our conditions if the human population don't mind eating tumor infested chicken? And I know there's that smaller human population who'll pay more for healthy chickens. But, lawd Jesus, look who gets to live range free and hormone free with all the green and clean air you can imagine? Them white... Foster Farms chickens!

Now you ain't ever gonna hear them squawk one bad word about the humans, cause them white chickens gets airtime on the human television and corporate benefits. I'm just testifying truth here. That's why them white chickens are scared of us project-borned chickens, cause we will peck out their eyes. And eat their gourmet worms. Bon appétit, bitches. Looking down their beaks like we love living in poverty. (*Singing.*) *Old MacDonald had a farm*... yeah, but that fool sold us all out to the factory farms! Nah, see, this shit got created long before I came into existence! Chicken or the egg, chicken or the egg, chicken or... (*She cough-clucks.*)

Goddamnit, I ain't supposed to be raising my blood pressure like that. (*Catche/s her breath.*) Lawd, that's better. Now, I heard, in some places, there are also poor white rural chickens suffering just like us. Lawd knows I don't wish these conditions on any kinda chicken, especially my own colored chickens I squabble with on the daily. Cuz as the Lord is my witness, we were all organic at one time, until the human came along. But it's like I tell my girlfriends, let them keep eating us. Watch them human babies, male and female, get breasteses and diabetes by age seven... we'll see who has the last cluck.

(CHICKEN *exits clucking. We hear ocean sounds as lights crossfade.*)

SCENE FIVE: SLICKSTER

[*A BIRD enters cawing. He has a plastic six-pack ring stuck to his leg. He swoops the area and then perches himself on top of the trunk. A moment later we hear the FISH humming a song. The FISH appears in "deconstructed form" swimming inside blue cloth. The FISH stops in dreaded fear when he spies the BIRD.*]

BIRD: Jesúcristo, what in the world happened to you, güey?

FISH: Japan.

BIRD: Hiroshima?

FISH: No, Fukushima.

BIRD: Ah, enough said, güey. Pinches humanos with their nuclear meltdowns and all these chingaderas that have been creating mierda en el mundo desde la Industrial Revolución. And I know, cuz mi abuela was drafted as a World War I pigeon carrier, and híjole, did she tell us stories. Como dicen, the early bird catches the worm, vámonos.

FISH: (*Moving away from BIRD.*) No... please, no!

BIRD: Oye, ¿qué traes? (*Slicks his feathers back.*) Don't be ascared. I'm not a real Mexican greaser. (*Points to head.*) B-P. Mira, I was dipping my beak in the Gulf of México and got sucked in by a black ola of

	chemical gunk. Oye… y oíste, Transocean gave all of those executive *caw* brones big bonuses for their "safety" record.
FISH:	No!
BIRD:	N'ombre, carnal, I've tried to get rid of this oily look. Bueno, it worked for the young John Travolta, ¿qué no? Then again, an Italian stallion gets more breaks than any burro mexicano I've ever met.
FISH:	Ha! I vas told my transport to the trial vas going to happen by mule. A vegetarian mule!
BIRD:	¡No mames, güey! Is that what they tole you? You didn't get the latest update? (*He pulls out a paper wrapped around his ankle and hands it to the FISH.*) A sus órdenes, señor. (*BIRD pulls out another paper and reads.*) Or as they say in your country… dangsin-ui seobiseu e.
FISH:	That is Korean. Very bad Korean.
BIRD:	Chingao, that's what I get for using Google translate.

(*We hear the drums from "Sorrow in Desert" by Kodo & Tan Dun. Suddenly, the FISH attacks the BIRD with self-defense moves. The BIRD retreats a bit. Music slowly fades out.*)

FISH: You eat fish!

BIRD: Woah... sí... cada vez en cuando, but in the big cities, it's more like left over Mickey D burgers, french fries, and those apple turnovers. Güey, is that what has you pissed off? Claro... (*Hand over chest*). I'm here to serve the animal revolution, and in revolución, carnal, (*raising his fist*) one must always put aside his personal needs and desires in order to serve the collective good.

FISH: Yes, yes, because as one of your Mexican revolutionaries once said, "It is better to die on your feet than to live on your vings!"

BIRD: Eso, y mira, no offense, pero even if it is my natural birthright to eat you, Señor Pescado, you would not be my first choice for dinner. I'm dealing with enough health issues, güey, I don't want to add radiation poisoning to that list.

FISH: Yes, of course, Mister Bird. Plus, in my old age, I vould not be very tasty. Just the other day, I vent to visit my great great great nieces and nephews in their school, and I told them, "Uncle is about to take a long journey in hopes that our oceans vill one day be clean again." Mister Bird, never vould I imagine swimming the entire globe just to speak in front of an international court of law. To tell the vorld vhat it vas like to vitness radioactive iodine coming at us like a giant fog. How in seconds I saw my lifelong friends and family choking and disintegrating before my very eyes. My husband and I swam as fast as ve could. "Shinjiro, swim deep down into the black vomb of the ocean for protection!" (*Catching his breath.*) Vhen I stopped to catch the oxygen in my gills... only a sliver of his shiny scales floated by... like glitter in the vater. He vas a poet. He vould have appreciated even the beauty in that. Gomen nasai.

BIRD: (*Wiping his eyes.*) Ay, carnal, I get it. I get it from above and below! Chingue su madre, can you imagine the kind of pollution we've been breathing in up there? They've put holes in the pinche ozone layer?! What kind of *animal* even does that? But this is why things have been changing, since 2012. We will prevail!

FISH: Yes!

BIRD: (*Pulls out a card.*) Y para que sepas, I'm also a card-carrying member of the gay aviary club. So joto to joto, trust, carnal, that your brave journeying and testimony will help to win our landmark case.

FISH: Yes, yes, you are right, Mister Bird. Let us finish this last leg of travel. From the Pacific Ocean to this Los Angeles River and now flying to New York City! I've always envied those flying fish. (*Hops in front of BIRD*) Vait 'til I tell the kids! Mister Bird, do you think I vill get jetlag?

BIRD: N'ombre, carnal, you won't get jet lag at all.

(BIRD eats FISH. Lights crossfade. We hear, "Testify" by Rage Against the Machine. BIRD pulls out a notepad and pencil. He slowly scratches out a name on his notepad. He grins. Does a mob pit-like dance. Exits. Lights crossfade again. We hear a subway in motion. The ROACH crawls onto stage.)

SCENE SIX: DOG IN MOVEMENT

[ROACH *practices her speech.* LADY FRIJOL *enters sniffing the air.*]

ROACH: We have heard testimony... no, no, we have heard *compelling* testimony—

LADY FRIJOL: Hello, there. Excuse me, I couldn't help but overhear... are you speaking at The Law of Mother Earth Trial?

ROACH: Yes, I'm actually the lead attorney for our case against Monsanto and other human corporate greed. Now that Mother Nature can act as a sole entity, in much the same way human corporations have been doing for decades, we can finally nail those human bastards!

LADY FRIJOL: That's bloody fantastic! You must be honored. My name is Lady Frijol, well, that's my colonized name. I've just started using my new name, Cihuatl Itzcuintle. As you can hear, I've been taking Chicana elocution classes. (*Chicana accent*) ¿Quiéres una cerveza (*British accent*) o un burrito? I'm still working on it.

ROACH: Nice to meet you. My name is Ms. Racha. Cuca Racha.

LADY FRIJOL: I know! Nice to meet you. I'll definitely be there for the closing arguments tomorrow. Is there anything I can help you out with?

(*LADY FRIJOL approaches her.*)

ROACH: Yes, please keep your distance! You'll alert a human to my presence!

LADY FRIJOL: Ah, yes, of course. Sorry. (*Beat.*) I would love to be of any other help. I'd've loved to have given my testimony. I offered up my story when the call of the wild* went out for the class action lawsuit, but I wasn't selected. Anyway, I can't wait to connect with other animals from the movement. Maybe we could meet up later for a treat? (*LADY FRIJOL approaches again and ROACH hisses; LADY FRIJOL moves away.*) I'm staying near the U.N. building —

ROACH: I'm sorry, but I really need to finish the edits on my closing argument.

LADY FRIJOL: Yes, of course, maybe tomorrow after your speech?

ROACH: The truth is, canine, most of us don't have the privilege of human allies who put us up at swanky hotels. If you haven't noticed, most of us don't use movement work as an opportunity for vacationing or sightseeing.

LADY FRIJOL: First of all, if you haven't noticed, I'm blind. So I'm not here to sightsee. Secondly, I think our movement benefits from human allies.

ROACH: I'm not interested in the politics of assimilation. Now, please, if you don't mind.

LADY FRIJOL: Assimilation? No, I'm talking about coalition politics—

ROACH: And I'm talking about radical politics! Because until the day all creatures are treated equally and consistently under the law of nature, not under the arbitrary law of man, human institutions must be interrogated at all levels. Look, canine, I reside in a brown community patrolled 24-7 by brutal humans who kill and maim (*raises her injured arm*) my loved ones without regard. (*Holds belly.*) And to think that now my domestic partner and I have 300 future offspring to worry about. Because, although I have many legs, I learned too late it was more reason to be careful whom I spread them for. Not just the first flaco marijuano who serenades me with his pretty song... (*She begins to hum "La Cucaracha." LADY FRIJOL joins in, until ROACH stops abruptly*). Why am I telling you this?

LADY FRIJOL: Maybe you need a friend?

ROACH: Look, canine, we can have a real political conversation the day your species finds itself under the constant threat of annihilation by pesticides or (*hits floor*) chanclazo!

LADY FRIJOL: Look here, Sra. Cuca Racha, I know what it's like to be abused by a human. My first owner kicked me whenever he felt like it. He knocked the sight out of me! And I nearly died when he chained me up for days without food or water!

It was torture, do you understand? And then I almost didn't get adopted because I was too… well, I wasn't a cute puppy anymore, so I nearly had to face death again. So don't talk to me like I don't know oppression. (*Beat.*) Whatever happened to not ranking our oppressions?

ROACH: Oh, canine, I'm not ranking the oppressions. I'm ranking the privileges. We can't be blind to them.

LADY FRIJOL: That's bloody rude and what you're saying is a load of crap.

ROACH: Okay, fine, canine. (*She puts away her speech notes and approaches LADY FRIJOL.*) Your individual experience is a sad one, granted. I am sorry for your pain. But would you say it is the common experience of the general dog population to suffer at the hands of humanity? Or would you say that in general dogs benefit from the care and love of humanity?

LADY FRIJOL: Well, in general, I suppose—

ROACH: Yes or no?

LADY FRIJOL: Yes, we benefit, but—

ROACH: Well, that, canine, is an institutional privilege we cockroaches have never benefited from. Now let me ask you this, if I went over to your place— would I be welcomed or exterminated by your human?

LADY FRIJOL: I see your point, but—

ROACH: Yes or no? A-ha! And at the end of the day, canine, you do have a place to call home. I suppose if things get too difficult for you in the movement—you can always go back to your cozy home. Yes or no?

LADY FRIJOL: Yes, but—

ROACH: Well, canine, for the majority of us in the movement it is the only home we've ever known. I don't have enough legs to count just how many animals—not to mention plant species—have suffered extinction because of these humans. And every animal testifying here has put their life in even more grave danger! So, I'm sorry, but I don't have the privilege to ever stop fighting for our rights! Case. Closed.

LADY FRIJOL: Yes, of course. I didn't mean to offend you, I just... blimey, well, when you have consciousness and a little bit of privilege, it can be a lonely place. What I'm saying is at least you have your community. I would give anything to have that.

ROACH: Well, there's that old adage: sometimes what you're looking for is where you started. (*Subway stops.*) This is my transfer.

LADY FRIJOL: Good luck tomorrow, Ms. Cuca Racha!

ROACH: (*As she exits.*) Don't get separated from your human ally. New York City can be a "ruff" place for an outsider. And by the way, nice collar!

(*A few beats.* LADY FRIJOL *removes her collar. We hear "You Know You Want Me" by Pitbull as lights crossfade to spotlight.*)

*A play on words based on the novel The Call of the Wild by Jack London

SCENE SEVEN: WHAT! WHAT!

[PIG *goes to the downstage spotlight to testify.*]

PIG: What ! What! (Snorts) Oink, oink, mother fuckers. Yeah, I swear to tell the whole fucking truth—I'm an atheist! Yo, pero if it makes you feel better, I'll swear on the entire Orisha pantheon de mi mamá. So, we cool, brode? Cuz, yo, check it out. Since it was fucking hurricane season estaba hangeando low in my Miami pig pen-house, when outta nowheres, these fucking come-mierdas grabbed me by the orejas and took me to the Guantanamo Bay! Years later, I'm thinking more like the agüantándome bay! And I told those come-pingas, "Oye, don't I got prisoner rights? Animal rights? Coño, I aing even political. I'm just a ghetto superstar. (*Poses.*) Yo, you probably heard my latest reggaetón hit, "When Pigs Fly." By yours truly, El Cochino. (*Poses.*) Cuz when it comes to Latin cuisine, I'm the one who put that Cuban sandwich on the culo-nary map. Just ask my worldwide fan base, you fucking come-pingas!"

Yeah, I squealed that mad shit in their human faces. Bueno, they had my patas tied with ropes and my mouth gagged with an apple, pero, you best believe that's the shit I was screamin' in my head, brode. Seguro. Cuz when the whole cochino thing took over the human mass media creating fear and pandemonium or should we say pan-pneumonia…? "Oye, singaos, don't look at me cuz you got the swine flu! Wash your hands, fuckers. What! What!"

And just cuz we cochinos like to fuck, everybody was looking at us horny pepperonis, like we spread the fucking killer virus. (*Beat.*) Pero, yo, check it out. I know who, how and why the whole swine flu outbreak happened. Mira, historically speaking the human empire targets the good-looking animales. Why you think they made that movie and called it, *Babe*? Pero, coño, look how they always be publicizing that shit: first, it was the *black* rats and the *Oriental* flea with the plague; then it was the mad cow disease—and we know during that slaughter the vacas were primarily *brown* and *black*; then it was the *Asian* birds with the SARS, and, last but not least, the *Mexican* pigs with the swine flu!

And, yo, I aing even Mexican! So why the fuck did they grab me? And I aing hating. I aing an anti-Castro puerquito. As a Communist pig, I'm down for revolution. So I aing got shit against other cerdos be they Mexican or Chicano or even that yuma, Ms. Piggy. Coño, in the end, all of our pig lineage actually hollas all the way back to Asia! How you think you get the chino in cochino? And even more retardum— have you heard how the humanos call my ancestors wild boars? How the fuck can I be wild and bore you at the same time?!

Pero, yo, check it out. My inside sources also told me that during the last *alleged* swine flu epidemic the numbers were exaggerated by the Centers for Disease Control—¿me entiendes? Just so in the end, some major pharmaceutical companies could make billions, brode, on some vaccine most humanos didn't even need. Coño, that's how we know the swine flu was just another conspiracy by the human empire to make our animal kingdoms look like villains, i.e. they want to murderize us all! What! What! Laboratory testing ain't enough?!

And, yo, I don't know about you guys, but my moms read me *Animal Farm*. I know what they said about us puerquitos not being able to cooperate together. We gotta unite, brode. It's what my música is about, even if I use cochino lyrics to lure the mamis... and the papis. You feel me, brode? Yo, cochino, I bet you wanna feel me. (*To audience member.*) You Mexican, brode? Cuz if he is... then we know he loves to suck on pig's feet! Oink, oink, mother fuckers. Yo, I know, I'm a fucking ham. Pero, you know you love my Cuban swagger. Pitbull aing got shit on me. Oye, he aing even a real pitbull! Fucking poser. "Oye, humanos—eat me!" They wish.

Gracias, you guys have been a great fucking jury. Yo, if she exists, may Yemayá bless you all. Oye, and, humanos, one last thing: Hands off Assata, mother fuckers! What! What!

(*Exits. We hear "Riding" by Chamillionaire. Lights crossfade.*)

SCENE EIGHT: SOUL MEMORY

[*TURTLE pokes her head from behind the curtain. Eventually, she enters with CATALINA on her back. Yes, this is a parody of the infamous YouTube video with the kitten riding the turtle. But here, CATALINA has an old-school water bottle over her belly. The "Riding" song crossfades to lesbian sex sounds.*]

CATALINA: Why is my Judy making those loud and terrible sounds? She's going to wake up the kids. What's that smell?

TURTLE: Copulation. But it's between our female masters, so it won't increase the population. (*CATALINA meows.*) Sex.

CATALINA: Grandma Turtle, do *you* do this thing… sex?

TURTLE: Not since Alfajiri, my owner, brought me here. We were both young back then. But before I was a respectable elder, I guess you can say I was a bit of a wild thing in Tanzania. Where would the biodiversity of the world be without nature's innate slutty behavior? Trust me, feline, me and polysexual Alfajiri won't be here longer than a weekend.

CATALINA: Vale, but it's been nice to have company, especially since… Grandma Turtle, do you ever get lonely?

TURTLE: Feline, humans do not think twice about separating us from our families. I am one of the lucky ones who came here in Alfajiri's Louis Vuitton New

Age Traveler backpack, solely because she's the daughter of a diplomat. Otherwise, I could have suffered the typical fate of African turtles that get stolen and shipped illegally in conditions so vile, most of us die en route. I have had to make peace with the fact that I will never see my family and friends again. And I will never have sex with another turtle.

CATALINA: That's so sad. Wait, so sex is making loud noises together?

TURTLE: (*Laughs.*) Noooo, feline! It's much more than that. The noise is the manifestation of the heat that burns in your groin and consumes your whole being. (*Responding to CATALINA's excitement.*) But, feline, you will not be having any sex or offspring for that matter. They cut the fire straight out of you.

CATALINA: (*Looks at "X" taped over her belly as she removes the heating pad.*) That's what getting spayed means…?

TURTLE: It's the norm for domestics. Population control. (*CATALINA starts to pace on all fours.*) Feline, what is happening to you?

CATALINA: Mi… corazón… fast…

TURTLE: Feline! Look at me… Feline! Look. (*TURTLE starts to sway her head to hypnotize her. CATALINA follows her motions.*) You are getting sleepy… very… very… sleepy.

CATALINA: I am? Maybe I'm just getting motion sickness... (*Looks like she might vomit.*)

TURTLE: No, feline, look! Look! (*She grabs CATALINA's attention again.*) Now count backwards. (*CATALINA turns around "backwards" and repeats the numbers as she crawls.*) 10-9-8-7-6-5-4-3-2-1... (*CATALINA falls into a deep sleep.*) What ills you, feline?

CATALINA: (*Her body twitches twice before she rises with a start, her eyes closed the entire time as she "purges" the following monologue.*) 1928-I am a Native girl, a child who will barely reach puberty when they come for me. Canadian officials will sterilize entire tribes. 1944-In Puerto Rico, I will have "la operación." For decades, a third of our female population will endure forced sterilization by the U.S. Empire. 1965-I will be poor again, so you can count me among the one million women who will be sterilized by the Brazilian government. 1978-I will have three children and live in South Dakota, when under false pretenses my ovaries will be removed by the Indian Health Services, heavily funded by the Rockefeller family. Over forty percent of Native American womyn will suffer from this illegal eugenics policy. 1986-I will be a black womyn living in Alabama when the white doctors from Medicare will coerce me into having a hysterectomy, shaming me by saying I already have too many children I can't afford to feed. Never mind they denied me two previous abortions when I asked for them! 1994-In Tijuana, all of us will line up in the morning and we will be required to swallow a migraine-inducing birth control pill or lose our jobs at the NAFTA maquiladora. 2000-In Peru and through President Fujimoro's "Voluntary Surgical Contraception" policy, I will be among the 300,000 rural Quechua womyn sterilized. 2013... (*She flails as if being beaten and then stops.*) At my local Chinese family planning office, when I petition for chronic pain relief from the first forced sterilization surgery I underwent eighteen years ago, authorities will beat me black and blue. They will call it a self-inflicted suicide.

TURTLE: (*Trying to bring her back.*) There, there.

CATALINA: But my real cause of death will rank me among the thousands of women murdered daily in this world and without justice.

TURTLE: There, there.

CATALINA: Grandma? Grandma? (*Lights back up. CATALINA retches. It takes her a moment to recognize her surroundings.*)

TURTLE: There, there. You're okay, little feline. You just experienced what the ancients call soul memory.

CATALINA: (*Touching her belly.*) They've... done this to me before? (*TURTLE nods*). And Lady Frijol was right, I was human in my previous lives? (*TURTLE nods.*)

And my past will be my future, unless... (*CATALINA gets very anxious again.*) I'm sorry, Grandma, I think I need to be alone right now.

(*TURTLE places her hand on CATALINA, shows her some kindness and ensures CATALINA is calm again. Then she starts to exit.*)

TURTLE: Little feline: haki zeto leo.

CATALINA: Grandma... I don't understand, Swahili.

TURTLE: "Our rights today."

(*Exits. CATALINA's tears continue to fall. She finds her anger and meows loudly, eventually removing her collar.*)

SCENE NINE: RAT RACE

[*Walking with his cane, the RAT takes his place under the spotlight.*]

RAT: I do promise to say de trut. What, yuh don't trust a rat? So help me, Jah Rastafari. Ya mon, I do believe we can bring down de human dic-tators... but we got to organize n unionize! Yuh know why de humans can manipulate us de way dey do? 'Cause everyone so happy with de little piece of cheese-cake, no mind dey pumpin de poor cows day n night like dey at a local gas station... I got me cheese-cake, what de fuck do I care bout some cow in a dangerous factory dat can fall on him, right? Wrong! Dat's de human mentality, God, we are better n smarter dan dat!

If you're not dey pet, yuh really tink dat a human has eva given a fuck bout yuh or me? I'm a rat working day in n day out to feed his family. I'm on dat subway too, traveling up n down dis island like de Wall Street crooks... except I can go home wid a conscious. Me not de reason yuhr home got foreclosed! N den do yuh know what dey have de nerve to call der own criminal kind? Dirty rats! Me not dirty! Me just black!

N den yuh see how dem humans get all teary eyed wid de *white* polar bears? "Ooh, de poor white polar bear stranded on a melting sheet of ice..." Ras, come to Brooklan in de peak of summer n I'll show yuh meltin. N why am I hating? I ain't even ever met a polar bear. Becoming just like a human n losing my decency.

Dere was a time in dis country when a rat could join a worker's union n get a decent job wid benefits alongside humans. In fact, de last decent human being on dis earth was de great Michael Jackson (does the iconic Jackson "hee-hee" sound). N coincidentally, de movie *Ben* was de last unionized job a rat could get regardless of his color or his sexuality. Me not gay, but I support me gay relatives, be it de mouse or de brown rat. I even support gay polar bears, as long as dey not acting white.

All of dis is de reason why to dis day I'm a rativist. Dere's a landfill of issues to take up. I tink back on all dat sacrifice n how my granparents really believed dey could find true balance n harmony *with* de humans, like de ancient days when tings weren't so fucked up n backwards. Ethiopia! Ya mon, we rats were even willing to put de past behind us – when we took de wrap for de Bubonic Plague... oooh, de scary *Black* Death. Beware, de dirty rat! Bambaclots, yuh know who was dirty? De idiot Europeans who never took a bath. True, why yuh tink dey invented perfume?

N for yuhr information, dat disease was not brought on by me kind, it was de pesky flea my ancestors carried on dere backs. N listen to dis...

dis is what nobody ever talk about. Dat plague killed so many of de working population dat it was de first time in Western history dat wages rose significantly. Major turning point in European economic development. Yuh see what I'm saying right? Dat plague made de human workers realize dey were *valuable*, all of dem.

But, I look round me, at dis fast-paced city, what dey call de "rat's race," n I tink, dat's what's wrong with dese humans, if dey cyan understand each other's value, how de hell can dey value anyting else? Tank yuh, yuhr Honor.

(*He starts to exit as lights go to black and we hear Usher's "OMG".*)

SCENE TEN: RAISING THE QUEER BAR

[*In silhouette the BUNNY does a mini-dance routine provocatively with his carrot. He never stops moving or hopping around in the scene. LADY FRIJOL enters with a KFC bucket and two beer bottles.*]

LADY FRIJOL: Strike me pink!

BUNNY: Vow, this hip-hop music is too good! Look at that gorgeous seahorse... oh, no, somebody already impregnated him, too bad.

LADY FRIJOL: The food at this party is delicious! This is the life! I'm telling you, Bunny, I was asleep, asleep like a damn rock most of my dog years. Bugger, but not anymore... hey, do I hear that bloke from the news? Yes, it's that bar fly, Anderson Pooper. I'm so glad that fruit fly finally came out of the closet.

BUNNY: Doggie friend, don't be so easily impressed. He's just one more celebrity vho came out only after he made his fame and fortune! Oh, look at that trans frog. I'd love for that tongue to flick my furry ass. (*Hops.*) Eh, baby, vhere is your lily pad? I love to do this thing on the vaterbeds. Let me guess... Detroit, Lake Michigan? (*Points to himself.*) Chicago! Ve're practically neighbors! I am telling you, you should thank this toxic pollution that gave you this extra eyeball, now you can see me properly, eh? Vhere you going?

LADY FRIJOL: I never would've imagine myself here. In the Animal Revolutionary Underground Party. So how many years have you been organizing?

BUNNY: Five. And I've fucked almost everything in this room, except that fine-ass donkey from Peru. (*Hops.*) Hee-haw, hee-haw, is right, mere jaan! (*Rejected again.*) I am telling you, doggie, your gender-benging is one thing, but interspecies dating is the vave of the future.

LADY FRIJOL: Yes, probably… I do feel the tides of change up on us, my friend. I can't wait to hear the closing arguments from Señora Cucaracha.

BUNNY. She is a liar! (*LADY FRIJOL makes a sound.*) A sell out. Don't get too hopeful. She's more human-identified than she lets on.

LADY FRIJOL: Who's a sell out?

BUNNY: Cuca. All of her kind for that matter.

LADY FRIJOL: Bollox! How can you say that?

BUNNY: I have heard this thing straight from the horse's mouth… (*enacting the following with carrot*) just before I put my carrot in it. (*Neighs in ecstasy.*)

LADY FRIJOL: But… but… this gathering is about making real change. So the humans are forced to remember their place in the web of creation.

BUNNY: Doggie, she is no better than any other diplomat. On the down-low, there is a story going around that she is going to accept a settlement from the human corporations. Doggie, just you think, vho benefits most from the human vaste?

LADY FRIJOL: I suppose you have a point.

BUNNY: The other thing I heard is that ve have so many of those Neo-Cointelpro enemies from vithin. Over 75 key vitnesses never made it to New York City, everything from primates to gut vorms to fish. They just vanished. For all I know, doggie, you could be micro-chipped... (*Moves away from him.*) Anyvays, everyone knows cockroaches have those European aspirations.

(*LADY FRIJOL makes an audible sound questioning this assertion.*) Yes, the cockroach vas once a guest of great honor in European homes, and it vas customary to release them in the new dwellings. Idiot humans thought it vould give them good luck. They did not know the roach is the nastiest critter of all. If you vere to ask me, the roach, the fly and the rat, should all be shipped off to the Maldive Islands vhere they can prosper in the dumps feasting on feces. Leave the rest of us decent animals alone. (*Puts his arm around LADY FRIJOL.*)

LADY FRIJOL: Most animals take a liking to feces.

BUNNY: Oh, yes, doggie, during pillow talk that same horse tole me that your kind loves to eat feces.

LADY FRIJOL: It's the oats. It's good for our digestive system.

BUNNY: Sure, vhatever you say, you kinky bitch. Look, doggie friend, I'm not saying anything new. Everybody talks behind closed doors. (*Beat.*) Revolution is a moment, my friend. Now real evolution... that is a lifetime. (*Beat.*) My dream girlboy, an intersexed hyena. They are hotness! Silly hyena, vhy are you laughing? I am telling you, ve can role-play mythical gods from the *U-bunny-shads*... (*Exits.*)

LADY FRIJOL: (*Barks.*) Then why are we here giving and listening to testimony? Why do we gather and vote and participate in this masquerade of animal rights campaigning? Bunny? Bunny?! BUNNY!

(*LADY FRIJOL exits. Lights crossfade.*)

SCENE ELEVEN: HOMEGROWN RESISTANCE

[*CATALINA enters reading a radical leftist newspaper. She paces.*]

CATALINA: Oh my gato, why didn't I know these things? To think that the birds and fish of this mundo have more guts than my kind. (*Reading paper.*) "To protest the pollution of the skies and the waters both species staged mass suicides in the Midwest followed by the Redondo Beach and Ventura beach areas; stupefying local human authorities when thousands of dead bodies fell from the skies or landed on their shores." And what have we kitties done? (*She pulls out a cell phone*) Where's the recorder?

(*Taps it and begins recording*) Dear Diary: We kitties have no revolutionary backbone, only individuals who believe in American exceptionalism and make stereotypical films like *Garfield* or worse, commercials for Fancy Feast showcasing those elitist 1% kitties. Lady Frijol was right. I am a pathetic pussy. (*Puts the cell phone down.*)

No, I'm not. As I learned in therapy, I have to stop negative speak. Plus, I have knowledge now.
So, vale, I will stage my own protest in this very house. Starting tomorrow, I will pee outside my litter box. I will tear Judy's precious curtains. I will meow into the late hours of the night, until she is forced to let me go outside by myself! Until then, I will create my own Event Page for mi revolución.

(*Begins recording again.*) Dear Diary: I don't have to go to the other side of the world to win my freedom. I am living in my oppressor's house. I will win freedom on my own sovereign terms, by employing pro-active and affirmative action steps. Since she took away my instincts to hunt and fend for myself, she should feed me every now and then. And if you ever find your precious cell phone again, Judy, I hope my voice makes you shiver. (*Meow laughs. She yawns and turns off the recorder.*) But first, I will take a power catnap.

(*CATALINA covers herself with a blanket and changes underneath it into COYOTE.*)

SCENE TWELVE: DISTANT RELATIONS

[*The lights change and the soundscape of a busy New York City street rises. LADY FRIJOL enters, not paying attention to the surroundings. A homeless COYOTE growls at LADY FRIJOL.*]

COYOTE: Watch your step, ai! Or you won't live to see the moon of another night.

LADY FRIJOL: I'm sorry. Look, I can't see, see? I'm lost!

(*COYOTE sniffs LADY FRIJOL.*)

COYOTE: Where'd you get the chicken?

LADY FRIJOL: Chicken? Oh, yes, I'm sure I could go back to the party and get some for you, chap.

COYOTE: (*Frisking him.*) You're plump enough, obviously a kept animal. (*Pushes him.* Get back to your owner, ai, before I make you my bitch. (*He takes his glasses. Pushes him again.*)

LADY FRIJOL: Hey, I need those. Why are you being so mean to me? We're related, aren't we? Coyotes and dogs? We're cousins.

COYOTE: Related, but not the same, ai. (*COYOTE snaps at him. LADY FRIJOL yelps in pain.*) Your kind has no wild left in you (*COYOTE*) *pushes LADY FRIJOL who falls to the ground. LADY FRIJOL defends* himself against COYOTE coming at him with a viscous bark and growl. Beat.) That's good, puppy, you'll need that if you expect to survive the streets. Now get. (Returns the glasses to LADY FRIJOL.)

LADY FRIJOL: I'll stay right here if you don't mind. (LADY FRIJOL sits on ground.)

COYOTE: Who are you? Why are you here?

LADY FRIJOL: I was at the U.N. trial—

COYOTE: Ai, you're with those assholes!

LADY FRIJOL: Yes. No!

COYOTE: I gave up on them years ago. Never gave me a real voice at the meetings and when they did, no real action. Just one damn report after another. They don't think we're real nations. So, fuck the U.N.

LADY FRIJOL: Yes, fuck the U.N. Fuck everything. I don't know what's real anymore. (COYOTE looks at LADY FRIJOL. Sniffs him again and studies him. He pulls out a lighter and some rolled tobacco. COYETE takes a puff.) Is that marijuana?

COYOTE: No. It's not what you think.

(COYOTE hands LADY FRIJOL the rolled tobaco and then howls at the moon. His howl breaks into a ceremonial song, LADY FRIJOL listens. COYOTE stops howling.)

LADY FRIJOL: That's bloody beautiful.

COYOTE: You can have it. Use it when you need the help of the spirits.

LADY FRIJOL: You're in touch with the spirits? Lucky.

COYOTE: Sunka, haven't you ever loved? Be it other sunkas, your land, or your own traditional way of howling at the moon?

LADY FRIJOL: (*Thinking*) No, I can't say that I have.

COYOTE: Then you don't know the first thing about survival. Go home. You'll get killed out here. I've seen enough death in my life, cousin. You don't know much, but I sense you have a good warrior heart. (*He takes a puff.*)

LADY FRIJOL: I do worry a lot.

(*COYOTE chuckles, LADY FRIJOL does too. Beat. Something happens to LADY FRIJOL. He "sees." He removes his glasses and looks directly at the audience. The vision disappears quickly. LADY FRIJOL puts his glasses back on.*)

LADY FRIJOL: Why was I shown that?

COYOTE: We all have a role to play, sunka. Everything you're fighting for begins with the spirit. Remember that, and maybe you won't lose your way again. (*COYOTE tilts his head and listens. Sound Cue for Animal Control.*) Animal Control!

(COYOTE *starts to run and then stops, realizing* LADY FRIJOL *is paralyzed with fear.* COYOTE *gives* LADY FRIJOL *a push.*)

COYOTE: Run, sunka! Run! I'll distract them!

(COYOTE *exits offstage yipping.* LADY FRIJOL, *completely disoriented, takes a few steps in one direction then another. A spotlight lands on him. He raises his paws in surrender. Black out.*)

SCENE THIRTEEN: THIS BRIDGE CALLED HOME

[*CATALINA enters reading* This Bridge Called My Back. *LADY FRIJOL enters, exhausted. CATALINA senses LADY FRIJOL.*]

CATALINA: Perra, you're back! (*She hugs LADY FRIJOL and purrs.*) I heard Judy say they found you! (*Whispers*) By the way, I think she implanted us with some kind of tracking device. Bueno, how was it?

LADY FRIJOL: Beastly... but—

CATALINA: Aw, good, I'm so glad you're back. I have so much to tell you. First, Judy está como una cabra! Can you believe after a string of flings, she already found another girlfriend *and* moved this woman in along with her two dar de lata hamsters?! It hasn't even been a full human month! (*LADY FRIJOL passes her an old paper bag.*) Ooooh. ¿Un regalito? For me?

LADY FRIJOL: It's really nothing. Just a small thing.

CATALINA: All the way from New York City? You shouldn't have. (*She plays with the bag.*)

LADY FRIJOL: Catalina! (*CATALINA stops playing.*) The gift is inside the bag.

CATALINA: Meow. (*CATALINA opens the bag and lets the gift fall out, a toy mouse.*) ¡Qué fuerte! Esto cuesta un huevo. (*She meows with joy and immediately begins to play with her new toy. Then she suddenly stops.*)

Oh, wait, I almost forgot. Perra, I have a revolutionary plan. Granted, I'm not as world savvy as you are these days, but I am sure it will work. Because, mira, I've been reading and thinking and reading and thinking—which is exhausting enough—but now I am ready to take action. True, I don't even know my own gata lineage. Estoy en diaspurr. Unlike you, perra, no tengo papeles. But that does not mean my existence is illegal. I don't need any official human documents to tell me that I am a creature of this land and that I can migrate wherever the fuck I want. I just need to escape this prison.

LADY FRIJOL: Ah, yes, the idealism of youth.

CATALINA: No, I've also been having prophetic dreams!

LADY FRIJOL: Have you ever been in love, Catalina?

CATALINA: We don't have time for love. We have a revolution on our paws!

LADY FRIJOL: Maybe the revolution begins in here. (*Points to her heart.*)

CATALINA: Oh, great, another Berkeley neo-hippie!

LADY FRIJOL: No, Gloria Anzaldúa. "I change myself, I change the world."

(*LADY FRIJOL crawls to his water bowl where he drinks.*)

CATALINA: Yeah, but the world won't let you change, unless we change it! And she also said, and I quote: "Do work that matters. Vale la pena." (*LADY FRIJOL laps water and does not respond.*) Mira, Itzcuincle... (*LADY FRIJOL stops drinking water.*) I just need to know, are you against me? Or are you with me?

(*LADY FRIJOL looks out and rises. He barks, and after some struggle, slowly howls the COYOTE's ceremonial song as the lights fade to BLACK. LADY FRIJOL turns to CATALINA who realizes it's a song of resistance and joins with feverish enthusiasm. She stands next to LADY FRIJOL and holds her claws out as they howl and meow together.*)*

TO BE CONTINUED.

**In a production with a larger ensemble, more animals should join in from offstage toward the very end of the song.*

ADELINA ANTHONY is a self-identified Xicana lesbian multi-disciplinary artista. The themes in her works address colonization, feminism, trauma, memory, gender, race/ethnicity, sexuality, in/migration, health, land/environment, and issues generally affecting the lesbian/ gay/ bisexual/ transgender/ two-spirited communities. With 20 years of experience acting, directing, writing and producing for theater, Anthony has garnered numerous nominations, honors and awards.

One of her critically acclaimed solo plays, *Bruising for Besos*, has taken Anthony in a new and exciting direction, making a full transition as a writer-actor-director-producer for independent film. *Forgiving Heart*, her first short film as a writer-director is based on the teenage years of Yoli Villamontes, the protagonist of *Bruising for Besos*. The short film world-premiered at the Outfest Fusion LGBT Queer People of Color Film Festival's Gala Screening in 2013, and has been turned into its own feature length screenplay. In addition, Anthony's *You're Dead To Me* was written as a participant of Film Independent's Project Involve, and world-premiered at the L.A. Film Festival the summer of 2013. Because of her participation in Film Independent's Project Involve program, she was awarded the 2013 Sony Pictures Diversity Fellowship. Working with her current screenwriting mentor, Ruth Atkinson, Anthony is developing the feature screenplay, *But Not Buried*, which is inspired by the Project Involve short film.

Along with Marisa Becerra, Anthony is the co-founder/producer of the independent film company, AdeRisa Productions, based in Ventura, CA. The company is dedicated to producing bold, entertaining, and high caliber queer/trans people of color films—with an emphasis on X/Chicana stories. At the time of publication of this book, AdeRisa Productions is in the process of fundraising for its first feature film, *Bruising for Besos*. It is her intention to adapt *The Beast of Times* into an animated feature film in the future.

A prolific artist, Anthony has been recognized by her communities and critics as one of the leading solo performers of her generation. She has been featured in *Colorlines Magazine, Frontiers Magazine, Adelante Magazine, Lesbian News Magazine, Texas Monthly Magazine, Bitch Magazine, Queer Codex: ROOTED!* and other publications.

For more information on the artist visit: www.adelinaanthony.com or www.aderisaproductions.com.

D'LO is a queer/transgender Tamil-Sri Lankan-American theater artist/writer/comedian. He has performed and/or facilitated performance and writing workshops internationally. This year, D'Lo became a board member of Brown Boi Project. D'Lo is also the creator of the "Coming Out, Coming Home" writing workshop series, which have taken place with South Asian and/or Immigrant Queer Organizations nationally.

D'Lo's poetry and short stories have been published in various anthologies and academic journals, most recently: *Desi Rap: Hip Hop and South Asia America; Experiments in a Jazz Aesthetic; Troubling the Line: Trans and Genderqueer Poetry and Poetics;* and, *Close, Too Close: The Tranquebar Book of Queer Erotica*.

Aside from touring the university/college circuit with *D'FaQTo Life* (pr. defacto), D'Lo tours *Ramble-Ations: A One D'Lo Show*, which received the National Performance Network Creation Fund Grant inclusive of residencies in 9 U.S. cities and additional support from the Durfee Foundation Grant, and his full-length stand-up storytelling show *D'FunQT* (pr. defunct), which has toured internationally (San Francisco; New York; Manchester, UK; and, a 7-city tour in India and Sri Lanka) through the Prakriti Foundation and a Ford Foundation Travel Grant.

Recent collaborations include D'Lo's work as the sound designer for Cherríe Moraga's play *New Fire*, which premiered at Brava Theater and touring with Adelina Anthony on her 2-person show *The Beast of Times*. A documentary by Crescent Diamond based on D'Lo's life/work, called *Performing Girl*, recently won the best short documentary award at Outfest 2013 and he most recently was lead character Jesse for the short film *LIT* by Elena Oxman. He also appears in the new HBO series LOOKING as Taj, and Mikki del Monico's film ALTO.

For more information on the artist visit: www.dlocokid.com

OTHER KÓRIMA PRESS TITLES

Amorcito Maricón
    by Lorenzo Herrera y Lozano

Brazos, Carry Me
    by Pablo Miguel Martínez

Ditch Water: Poems
    by Joseph Delgado

Empanada: A Lesbiana Story en Probaditas
    by Anel I. Flores

Las Hociconas: Three Locas with Big Mouths and Even Bigger Brains
    by Adelina Anthony

Joto: An Anthology of Queer Xicano & Chicano Poetry
    edited by Lorenzo Herrera y Lozano

The Possibilities of Mud
    by J. Jiménez

Tragic Bitches: An Experiment in Queer Xicana & Xicano Performance Poetry
    by Adelina Anthony, Dino Foxx, and Lorenzo Herrera y Lozano

When the Glitter Fades
    by Dino Foxx

Made in the USA
Middletown, DE
27 March 2015